GOLD

With best wishes,

Elaine Feinstein

July 2000

Also by Elaine Feinstein from Carcanet

Selected Poems
Daylight

Elaine Feinstein

GOLD

CARCANET

First published in 2000 by
Carcanet Press Limited
4th Floor, Conavon Court
12-16 Blackfriars Street
Manchester M3 5BQ

A CIP catalogue record for this book
is available from the British Library
ISBN 1 85754 449 8

The publisher acknowledges financial assistance
from the Arts Council of England

Set in 10pt Palatino by Bryan Williamson, Frome
Printed and bound in England by SRP Ltd, Exeter

Contents

Acknowledgements

Some of these poems have already appeared in *The Times Literary Supplement*, *Poetry Review*, *Poetry Nation Review*, *Poetry in the Parks*, *Grand Street* and *Thumbscrew*.

In writing *Gold*, I drew on the expertise of Barbara Garvin Finler, of the Italian Department at University College London, da Ponte's own memoirs, and Sheila Hodges' biography, *The Life and Times of Lorenzo da Ponte* (1985).

Gold

1

A wintry gold floods the bedroom this morning:
a January sun, drenching the air, alight
in a silk scarf, a yellow flare in the mirror.
I used to revel in the glitter of night,
but, over here, the dark has little glamour.

Let me introduce myself: Lorenzo da Ponte.
Mozart would smile to see me here in America
weighing out tea or measuring a yard
of plug tobacco. I have bolts of cloth,
salt pork in kegs, sewing thread, waxed cord.

My customers are cobblers or carters.
They offer lame horses and watery cider
instead of money; I must be content
to scratch a meagre living as a grocer.
It is a mask I wear, and I have spent

most of my life in one disguise or another.
Living on my wits – *Se vuol ballare,*
Signor Contino – like my Figaro,
but always more of an interloper.
Where did I find the nerve to put my toe

over the baroque threshold of the feudal?
My father lived in the stink of untreated
leather, without comfort or property,
hoping for nothing more than our survival.
He knew nothing of Tasso or Dante.

And so was spared the evil whispers
behind the jewelled hands of gorgeous
ladies in the Imperial Court.
In Europe, the children of tanners
do well to remain tanners.

2

I remember three Empires, but
what do I recall by now of Ceneda?
Disorder, hunger, urine, cats in
the streets and all the usual clobber
of poverty, shoeless children, dirt.

If there were any men with fat purses
in that ghetto north of Venice, my father
was not among them, poor man, confused
by many creditors, he was no usurer,
but rather harshly used.

Ceneda put a sibilance in my Italian,
although I never learnt the stoop of
the older generation, and women,
I soon noticed, like my courteous
words, fine hands, and even

the stranger's darkness in my eyes.
D'ove sono i bei momenti. Yes,
lovely creatures, ill used by their husbands,
were generous to me. You hear their voice
in my sad aria for the Countess,

Mozart transfigured in his garden music.
D'ove sono i bei momenti? My pen
could race down pages, lickety-split,
writing of the unhappiness in women.
You will not find my words in Beaumarchais.

Here in Elizabethville, a girl with skin
of white milk and dimples, often
comes into my shop with a child
to collect her husband's medicine.
I know he bullies her. One day,

I saw a bruise under her eye. Before
my lips had framed the obvious question
her boy surprised me – *Mister, what happened
to your teeth?* She pulled him close
to hush him in his ear. I am a man

in late middle age, a little vain – toothless
or not – and scrupulously dressed.
I still walk upright, though I use a cane.
And briefly, I was tempted to confess
the flattering details of a scabrous story.

My Nancy was upstairs, however, making
her *capelletti Bolognese.* So,
for all my rumoured immorality, not a
tender word was spoken, though
she might have listened like a Desdemona,

and perhaps my snubs and humiliations
would then have gained the spell of an adventure,
as if I had chosen to live on the run.
Just as the very dust of the air in
sunshine takes on the lustre of sequins.

3

The teeth? Well, I'll come to that story later.
There's a more serious matter, which still grates
in my flesh like seeds of dirt in an oyster.
I wanted to live with a bit of flash and brio,
rather than huddle behind ghetto gates.

It's not a question of faith. What I wanted to do
I knew as soon as I started to read Italian,
learnt on my own from torn books in the attic.
And only poetry could work the magic
of changing me into a European.

My mother died before I was five. My father,
too distressed to comfort anyone, found teachers
who were ignorant of Latin. I was not content
to be excluded from the opportunity of
being a child of the Enlightenment.

Far from getting answers to my questions,
my brother and I were often whipped.
As for scruples of my ancient religion,
I learnt little of those beyond the script
of the Hebrew language, though

a few sayings entered my imagination.
If I am not for myself, as Hillel has it,
*who will be for me? And if I am
only for myself, what am I? And if
not now, when?* He was a poet.

When I was fourteen, my father wished
to marry a Christian girl. The price
was the conversion of the whole family.
Knowing so little of what I was to enter,
I thought Christendom must be Paradise.

There were drums beating, cathedral bells,
halberdiers in ceremonial dress, the Feast
of the beheading of St John the Baptist,
when I who was born Emanuele
Conigliano became Lorenzo da Ponte.

I knelt down to become a citizen, and
shoved my origins out of my mind. I thought
if a little water purified my hand,
my spirit could flow into the main stream,
whatever earlier generations taught.

It seemed a gift of fortune unalloyed
when the same Bishop, whose name we'd taken,
put my brother and I in a seminary. Buoyed
up by reading Petrarch, Ovid, Horace,
I became so crazily studious

I had no time to chafe at celibate life.
My mentors, sadly, thought me too ambitious,
and mocked my first verses. Those who find
in my behaviour only desire for material good
miss out my schoolboy trust in all mankind.

4

Venice was water and sky, barges
of musicians on the Grand Canal,
perfumes, fans, a fever of carnival.
On my first visit there, I fell in love
with the whole city: the shops open,

till midnight, shopkeepers singing
as loudly as gondoliers. I lingered
in bookshops and in coffee houses
talking to men of letters. On my first visit,
I won the reputation of a wit.

The next, I had my purse of coins stolen
and didn't care, since I could see beggars
able to relish singers and lanterns.
Alas, I was to blame in staying on, for
when my father's leather shop went under,

he'd urged my brother and I into the Church
to train as priests – and I did not resist.
For someone of my temperament, that mask
was one, at least, that should have been rejected.
A priestly vow is dangerous, if neglected.

To begin with, venal sins aroused little
opprobrium as such. How I behaved
with girls was altogether commonplace.
Voi che sapete . . . I was soon the slave
of Angiola, a ferocious beauty

who taught me all that was depraved
in pleasure, praising my precocity,
with delicate caresses, smiling to see
anxieties forgotten. She encouraged me
to think a little money might

keep our delicious nights alive for ever.
My friend Casanova, who was much colder,
more brutal – he devoured women like
sweetmeats – warned me her brother
was a well-known pimp but I took no notice

– Venice was a city of courtesans – though
sometimes glances that the two exchanged
held an affection something more than sibling.
I was too young, and did not want to know
what in the outcome had me half deranged.

So I joined their gambling in taverns.
Once a good hearted gondolier lent
me a few coins, and that won others, so
for a time I became Angiola's mascot.
The gift I gave back. And the rest we spent.

Now where, I wonder, did that fiction rise
that all my tribe are both wealthy and mean?
When on the Rialto, sometimes, I saw men
in beards wearing their gaberdines,
with sallow faces, I lowered my eyes,

in case they read my stare as one that mocked.
They were old, and sad, and if there lurked
among them any single, vengeful Shylock,
he would not cherish any hope of justice
within the noble Christian courts of Venice.

Infatuated, dissolute, poor, at last
I tried on a new mask; that of magician.
And since Venetians put some trust
in alchemy, for a time I prospered,
as if I were a licensed conjuror,

though naturally no gold was ever made.
The Church still took no interest in me.
It was as if I'd simply found a trade.
The role was one I might even have played
for longer, if one afternoon I had not

found my sweet Angiola in our bed
with two men, entertained lasciviously.
Challenged, she threw an inkpot at my head.
I had no choice. I picked up a few clothes.
That very hour, without much dignity

I left the city in a jealous temper,
making for Treviso, where I could
earn some money as a Latin teacher,
while writing a few poems on the need
for human beings to behave as brothers.

My politics at the time were innocent.
I did not imagine much original
in what I wrote, almost as exercise.
The morals I approved were Roman, decent;
but looked seditious to an Abbot's eyes.

And I was in the Church. All of my past
actions were examined in a new light.
I stood accused as gambler, fornicator,
adulterer and rapist, though that last
for my own pride I must deny.

Those poems brought me to the attention
of the Venetian Senate. The Inquisition
was soon investigating my conversion.
I did not stay to argue the position,
but left sweet Venice quickly for Trieste.

5

And what to do next? My brother's income
was, I well knew, committed to support
my father and the family. From now on,
the Church banned my employment as teacher.
Was I condemned to living as a con man?

Not my intention, but I'd have to busk it.
I was outside Venetian jurisdiction, but
the Church has a long arm, as well I knew,
and even to earn my bread I dared not risk it.
You cannot always recognise

the good news from the bad. I might,
without that incident, have spent
my whole life in a dingy backwater.
Instead, it was to Dresden that I went
to see an old friend, who was Court poet

to the opera. He knew I had some talent,
though while I hung around he did
little to further it. It was only
the morning I was on my way
the fellow seemed suddenly to relent,

as if sure then of no awkward demands.
He scribbled a few lines to Salieri
in Vienna: 'Do for him everything
that you would do for me.'
And with that letter a new life began.

6

Enough. You want to hear about Mozart.
How did he live? Who were his favourite women?
Did he have any secret habits, stuff
he put in Tokay, or snorted with his snuff?
As if what genius does for recreation

has much to tell us about what he is.
I can only say: I loved the man,
and if you wonder what I had in common
– apart from laughter and frivolities –
with such a genius, famous since he was six,

I'd say: though I was a late starter
we rapidly gained the same enemies
– Casti, for instance, syphilitic, burring
through the wreckage of his nose –
as both of us hustled on the peripheries.

In Vienna, nothing counts but rank.
A Baron with a house in Herrengasse,
and all his land in hock, still keeps a gig
painted with family insignia, his wig
is well cut, and his clothes elegant.

That's Empire for you. And always, at the centre,
toadies will prosper more than any talent.
Which is not to say I couldn't flatter
but even at the height of my acceptance,
the snobbish flunkeys always had my measure.

Still, there were pretty milliners, dressed
in feathers, cafés on the Graben.
At first, I took up lodging with a tailor
near Taborgasse, where the market stalls
sold trinkets, hot potato cakes, and shawls,

and settled in, before taking my letter
to Salieri in the First District. Naturally
I greeted him at once as an Italian,
while he read over what I'd brought, with caution.
I didn't mention my priestly career,

but said I had a Bishop as a godfather.
On some matters, I had to stay alert,
if not evasive, since the Emperor's mother
in her lifetime had allowed no Jews, convert
or other, to live in her Vienna.

Salieri introduced me to the Emperor;
I was appointed to the Italian Theatre,
and on that stage discovered my true home.
The make believe delighted me at once:
I loved the candle starlight, painted domes,

the filmy, shimmering clothes, and feathery wings
which transformed actors into gods and kings.
That said, the only people there who prosper
in opera houses are the leading singers.
They hold the rest to ransom: scene shifters,

tailors, extras, engineers, composers
and poets always bottom of the pile.
Salieri was witty and versatile,
but my first opera, let me confess,
– with his music – was not a success.

The Emperor was kind about my failure,
encouraged me to try my luck again;
when the next went well, he whispered
to me: *Abbiamo vinto*. So I was in favour.
For a time, could use green porcelain

to eat my breakfast, sit on lacquered
white chairs with goats' feet, wear
an ankle length coat of Chinese silk,
and be a guest in the Imperial palace,
though I might well fear poison in the chalice.

When I was ill, I warmed my bed with embers
in a copper pan, drank claret and madeira.
I worked for anyone: Martin y Soler,
Martini, Storace. Whoever asked.
I learnt my trade as I performed the task.

Is it a serious art to write libretti
when so few people listen to the words?
Those who found me glib, would often say
I did no more than *translate* poetry,
and steal the shape of better writers' plays.

Beaumarchais himself was rather kinder.
He said *The Marriage of Figaro*, cut
into our version, was a miracle, and that
to turn a five act play into an opera
was of itself to make a new drama.

When Mozart wanted to set *Figaro*, the play
was banned in Austria, I dared suggest
I knew exactly what could be hacked out.
And Emperor Joseph let us have our way.
It was a risk, but somehow I had guessed

that in that chance lay immortality. I changed
Figaro's first name, for superstition:
Beaumarchais had him as Emanuel,
which was my own name before baptism.
I wanted no gossip about my religion

– as if that would ever dwindle away.
There were many around us who were jealous,
not of my skills, of course, but Mozart's genius,
and they included Salieri, my first patron.
It was stupid of me, then, to start a liaison

with a singer that he thought belonged to him.
In those days I was rash, and handsome,
with all my teeth. Ah yes. I promised you
that story. I have never been quite sure
how much what followed had to do with him.

A girl where I lodged had dismissed her lover,
praising my good looks. I hardly knew her,
or the rejected lover, save as a surgeon,
till I met him in a coffee shop, and mentioned
one of my gums might have to be lanced.

'Cut?' he said. 'No need of that.
For a sequin I will rid you of the trouble.'
When he returned he had a blue glass bottle.
'Put this on your gums,' he said, 'with a cloth.'
And so I did, and thanked him for his skill.

My nature at the time was not suspicious.
I was putting on the lotion with a placid
hand, obedient to instructions, without
a thought of any danger, when
my maid screamed out: 'Jesus, that's nitric acid!'

– she often used the stuff for washing clothes.
I did not doubt her, rinsed my mouth at once
with vinegar and milk. The harm was done.
And in a few days my gums were wax.
On the left side my teeth dropped one by one.

They didn't take to *Figaro* in Vienna.
We had to wait for Prague. One day,
along the Graben, I met Casanova.
I was feeling low, since hearing that my brother
– abler than me and far more virtuous –

had fallen ill and died. I cursed whatever
powers muddle up God's justice.
My friend and I fell into each other's arms.
Although we'd quarrelled long ago in Venice,
I never wished the fellow any harm.

We dined that evening with a pretty dancer
and La Ferarrese, an opera diva
of whom you will hear more. In Grinzing
we ate roast goose and drank champagne together.
Soon after, I was afire with *Don Giovanni*,

and put the plot of it in front of Mozart.
He liked it, and I've never written faster.
I kept awake by taking Seville snuff,
a girl of sixteen sitting close enough
for me to fondle, when my ink ran dry.

And then it was a tranquil Prague October.
I recall autumn leaves, and birdshell skies;
in an old farmhouse Mozart and Constanze
stayed – I have never heard such birdsong –
while I lodged opposite the three Lions.

We were still doing re-writes that week,
so I was involved in the rehearsals,
but Mozart would not write the overture.
The more we pleaded, the more he was playful.
At last, we tricked him into the Bertramka

and locked him in upstairs with his piano.
Seeing us through the window, he spoke
fretfully of being left alone. We passed up wine
and baked meat, begging him resign
himself to work, and then he took it as a joke,

and with relief we heard the first notes
of the score. A coachman took me home.
That night I walked about the city,
enjoying Prague, and gossiping with Czechs
whose late night badinage was wry and witty.

Their theatre goers favour the dramatic.
They have a legend of an ancient monster
haunting the stones of the Jews' cemetery,
but they are my ghosts, the dead who lie there,
and, if unquiet, they don't frighten me.

It was my touch to have the father's statue
return for his revenge, though Mozart
blenched at it. He felt some guilt, I knew,
for disobedience of his own father. I had
no fear of mine rising out of Hell

since he was still alive and short of money,
no apparition needed to remind.
In *Stavoske Divadlo*, that anxiety
quickly dropped out of my mind. It was
the prettiest Theatre I had seen.

And at the first performances, I gasped
to see the audience in their finery
and hear the bustle; I had never grasped
what listening to applause would mean to me.
I knew they'd loved our *Figaro*, of course,

but had not heard the clapping for myself
or felt elation stirring in my blood. Seeing
my own libretto, bound in gold paper
sold outside at 40 crowns a copy
seemed to authenticate my whole being.

The dialogue, the counterpoint, the melodies:
La ci darem la mano was my favourite.
Meanwhile composers, still using my libretti,
began to mock my ignorance of music,
and often said, you cannot trust a man,

who cannot even play a simple piano,
and makes his living out of writing opera.
He speaks too cleverly, glib, and so it is
that foolish women throw themselves at him.
La Ferrarese, say, who played Susanna

in *Marriage of Figaro*, during its revival.
She was my mistress, yes, although
she brought me to my knees more by her
singing than her beauty, her contralto
voice, teasing as well as pleasing.

I knew the substance of her reputation
– her jealousy, her street violence –
but, warned against the association
because she had so many enemies,
I became even more her partisan,

and gave her parts for which she was
unsuited. Meanwhile, many voices
spoke viciously of my collaboration:
in *Cosi fan tutti*. It was a gentle variation
on the old story of inconstant women.

Mozart's angelic harmonies transformed
my wicked plot, but there were moralists
who found me cynical, and warned
I could not be indulged inside the Court.
Salieri arranged most of the slanders.

Perhaps it was support of La Ferrarese
made me so unpopular? Her song
was out of fashion, and she herself was old
when our love ended. Something went wrong.
And soon the new Emperor, Leopold,

looked on me with so much disfavour
I had to leave the comforts of Vienna
for London, marriage and financial ruin.
But let me say, my bride was not the problem.
My Nancy had amazing acumen,

as well as youth and beauty. In my English
troubles – with an unscrupulous producer
whose notes I'd signed in rather foolish
fashion – Nancy was much shrewder.
She ran a coffee house and kept the profit

in her own name, until we sailed away
from Europe, debts and prejudice –
she was another convert, by the way –
to a New World over the stormy seas
where nobody recalls our histories.

9

To speak now as an enlightened ghost,
my end was better than you might suppose.
In New York, in a bookshop once, I met
by chance a man who loved Italian poets.
When he discovered what I knew by heart

he introduced me to his wealthy friends.
And even as Nancy and I entered society,
the Italian Opera with my *Don Giovanni*
was crossing the Atlantic. When it arrived,
I found that my celebrity revived.

My Nancy became a renowned hostess,
who carried herself with grace and, since
she spoke four languages, easily impressed
our new admirers. As for me,
I taught the treasures of Italian poetry.

Poor Mozart was so much less fortunate.
My only sadness is to think of him, a pauper,
lying in his grave, while I became
Professor of Italian literature.
Nobody living can predict their fate.

I moved across the cusp of a new age,
to reach this present hour of privilege.
On this earth, luck is worth more than gold.
Politics, manners, morals all evolve
uncertainly. Best then to be bold.

Lyrics

Living Room

How can we make friends before one of us dies
if you quarrel with two fingers in your ears,
like a child? Things won't come out right now.
You think I don't love you. I won't argue.
Your angry sadness stings me into tears.
I think of your old mac, smelling of chemicals,
leant against long ago in the 'Everyman' queue,

when you offered me those tender early
films that made our lips tremble, or else
the forgiven boy in the forest of Ravel's opera,
more touching to me than your verbal
skills or passion for the genius of gesture
in crayon, mime, *commedia del arte*.
It's love we miss, and cannot bear to lose.

I know you would much prefer I choose
intelligence to prize, but that has
always had its down side, your words
so often cut me down to size, I wonder
if some accident removed me first, whether
my writing days would count as evidence
that in my loss was little real to miss.

The likeliest end is that the bay tree left
to my attention, withers on the window sill,
and moths lay eggs in the lentils, while
still hurt by memories of you as gentle, I'll
look into a monitor for comfort, and cry
aloud at night in the hope somewhere
your lonely spirit might hang on and care.

Still Life
Out of a tale by Washington Irving

After your monstrous sleep, you woke lying
in the doorway of a shop selling bankrupt stock,
with two buskers and a pit bull guarding their tin;
a wintry city, the wind getting up, and ghosts in your head
that no one else remembers. In the window
you make out white bristles pushing through skin.

Bewildered, as if in the fairy tale, your back
sunk against old clothes, you mull over
what became of your life, what you might
have done, or could have, if not for
the spell that held you. Dozing,
you try to remember,

to hear the voice of your own working mind
against the rap of this millennial city,
where the biology of tenderness is forgotten
and the only ties are those of single
electrons forming bonds between
atoms in a craving for stability.

Paradise

Even the sad music from the car radio is glamorous
this morning, as I take the curve up the hill.
The sun glitters on rainy streets
like a shoal of herrings in water,
this early March tingles my blood
as yellow touches the strands of a willow:
a freedom intoxicating and dangerous.

No one knows where I am. No one
cares what I do. It's alarming
to be untethered as a kite slipped from
a child's hand, and then blown past
this high street of shop windows: Monsoon,
French Connection, Waterstones.

The last gives me pause. I wonder
whether it was cowardice or duty
denied me this pleasure so long,
to take comfort from the name on a book spine
or italic under a photo, while the blood
of my life found a pulse only in song.

After La Traviata

She calls *Too late* from her bed, and in fury
I feel the hot salt spilling out of my eyes,
as if her need to love undermined all witness.
One great cry, and we forget his mistrust,
her jewels sold in secret to pay their bills;
and lament only for happiness lost.

Yet even without the blackmail and bullying
of the father's intervention, Violetta's surrender
speaks of a passion foreign to our age, when
people are supposed to move off for their own good;
and friends to chivvy them out of such obsessions.
Why should she spend herself to the last cough of blood?

The tears give another answer. Looking around,
in the ENO audience, I see women weeping
on every side, as if such commitment arouses
a profound longing; we may refuse to be sacrificed,
but respond to the fiction, are betrayed
in the music, and not only in opera houses.

Casualty

A green computer called George is reading
my vital signs through a peg on an index finger.
I try to understand the bleeps, while the Ibo nurse
chuckles and gives his rusty stand a kick:
'This one, he's unreliable old thing.'

Four a.m. She leaves, and then it's lonely.
Even George has gone now, though eight leads
are still attached to my chest and legs. I'm
knackered, but I can't sleep on the trolley
and there's nothing here to look at but a shelf

of cardboard piss pots and an oxygen mask,
the bin for contaminated spikes, and a
red button to be pushed in asthmatic spasm.
Impatient for daylight, tossing in my cot,
thoughts rattle in my head: I want

my ordinary life back. What
a mistake to let an ambulance
carry me off to this wretched ward.
There may be nothing much wrong.
That sudden hope rises in me like birdsong.

Freedom

When you are out, I wander round the flat,
eat fruit, read newspapers and do
surprisingly less work. No doubt of that.

So what am I missing? Are you right to claim
a blown up effigy, sitting in a chair
would be the same?

Not quite. The poem's space may
seem to offer its own escape, but I still need
the goad of words that find their mark.

When I look down through glass
to see you getting out of a black cab,
frazzled, hair wild, and raincoat open,

fumbling for change, and know that
you are neither lost nor hurt – it's brief,
but what I feel is passionate relief.

Respite

Rain in the beech trees at 4 a.m.:
I ran away from your voice to
sit in an upright chair. Useless
in your despair, I had no
strength to scoop you
out of your long story,
let alone think of rescue.

Somewhere, the elfin child
of your tinted sepia photo
was still bravely smiling,
with a nail of ice in his heart.
And how can we be reconciled
to that, or hope to unfreeze
what has been so long frozen?

Then you struggled, on sticks,
to my side. You kissed my fingers,
and face, begging me back into bed,
calling me good and kind.
And generous words of love
flowed on all night long, as if
they healed your flashing mind.

Prayer for my Son

Most things I worry over never happen,
but this, disguised as an embarrassment,
turned risky in a day. Two years ago,
from the furthest edge of a blue sky,
an illness snatched his livelihood away.

Justice, Lord? How is this just? I
muttered, as if every generation must
learn the lesson again: there is
no special privilege protecting us.
He lay across his futon, white and thin

– the QEH sold out, his dep chosen –
in double torment. No one could comfort him.
I would have kissed the feet
of any holy man – as the Shunamite
woman did – to have the Lord relent.

But what since the miracle of his recovery?
Petty angers, like a girlish sulk. Forgive
me such ingratitude. Let him only live
with grace, unthreatened, on the sound of his flute
– and I'll stop clamouring for sweeter fruit.

Wasp

The Singleton is fiercer than the rest.
Who would have guessed?
A sleepy wriggle will provoke the thing.

My leg is swollen red with histamine.
Doctors say from now on I must live
in fear of another sting.

Immortal wasp, only last October
I put your crippled body out the window
and here you are again, buzzing with Spring.

City Lights
For Fisher at seventy

Roy, I'm fussed by festschrifts.
Even when I promise
a piece, I either miss
the deadlines, or the lines
themselves fall dead.

I learnt from you that poems
can be lit by zinc, and smell
of currants or petrol; I
walked the wet streets
of your city memories,

hearing that childhood sneer
of the Midlands in my ear:
'You *what*? You must be joking.'
In Cambridge, at the Erard,
yours was a nimble answer.

Dud keys sounded for your fingers.
Let me salute you then, as jazz man,
stand up comic, fellow poet, and
for many years my bookshop companion –
filed under F – as another outsider.

Exile
i.m. Andrew Kelus

It was what you wanted, your friend told me.
Your creditors had been anticipated.

They will not evict you now from your apartment
hanging over the river in Basel. Yet

it was your extravagance I loved, the absurd
gesture of taking us, with three children

for snails in garlic butter at the Rhinekeller.
It was a generosity you couldn't afford

even then, even before young men
and beautiful possessions had consumed

whatever you earned. I remember
once you took an army knife away

from a mugger working the New York subway,
because you had seen he was afraid.

I know that other people often paid
for your recklessness, but in defence,

you shared with them your own talent for
revelling in joy more than common sense.

Encounter

Afloat in October, my birthday month
in Baltic sunshine, my mouth satisfied
with coarse russet apples, their flesh
yellow rather than white, I lay down

to sleep where there was starlight
and the sound of water and dreamed
of the desert. There were leaf shadows
and watery light, and an unknown

presence in a pile of stones.
Whether the man who wrestled
with me all night long was good
or evil, he blessed me at first light.

In Praise of Flair

That whole wet summer, I listened to Louis Armstrong.
Imagined him arriving in New York after Funky Butt
dance halls, wearing hick clothes: those
high top shoes with hooks, and long
underwear down to his socks.

Thought of him shy in a slick, new band, locked
for two weeks reading the part he was set,
until the night when Bailey on clarinet
took over an old song. Then Louis' horn
rose in harsh, elated notes,

of phrases he'd invented on riverboats
and ratty blues tonks, using all the sinews
of his face and muscle of his tongue.
And what delights me now,
is when he grinned to thank

the crowd that stood to clap, and saw
slyly from the corner of his eye
all the stingy players in the band
were sitting motionless, their tribute
only an astonished sigh.

Options

Illicit one-time love, your face
was narrow as mine, Italian as
De Niro. You were fortunate
to escape marriage to me, yet
sometimes, I confess, you visit
my salacious dreams. I wear black
lycra above the knee, and meet
your eyes as if you were an eager
punter on Great Windmill Street

It's years since I gave back your rose cut
diamond ring – which doesn't show much wit –
so why would I think of calling you this evening
half way across the world? I have
your number, but see no point using it.
It's far too late for an alternative life.
You would have hated being strapped for cash.
And who can tell how long we would have
burned together, before turning to ash?

Snowdonia

Black on white, a roadside, a shock
of mountain rock: I am looking in
through a photo found in an Indian tin,
to a piece of my lost history.
There on my father's knee,
my hair cut like Clara Bow,
I can't have been more than three.

Do I remember, or is it a dream
that the group of relations, resting
on stones, are exhausted to mutiny,
while my father continues to urge us upward?
My eyes look shyly under my fringe
at whatever he wants me to see.

For a moment I imagine his voice.
'The air, taste the air.' And my throat
tightens, searching the square
of a black and white photo,
a band of ghosts, and a
mountain's majestic glare.

Boatsong

Looking at figures of flicked ink
trudging up hills of snow, their plan
panning for gold in the Klondike:
that is *one* mistake, I think
I was unlikely to make.

People usually choose the shape
of the dangers they undertake:
anchor men, traders in futures
dealers in crack cocaine
all select the style of their fear.

So what am I doing here?
On dark waters near Torquay
once as a child, I let myself drift
on a lilo out to sea,
and was lucky to survive.

Now in my study I sail along
trawling for words to feel alive.
And that is my rush of adrenalin
with muggy London air in the lungs,
and oil of wintergreen on my skin.

Galway

At the Breton restaurant in Galway
the claws of huge brown lobsters caught
in the Atlantic wave are still moving.
Do we lie to ourselves about everything?
They will boil slowly into restaurant red.

Two swans extend their necks in lines of muscle.
They live on fish here, not tourist bread.
And they, at least, are wild as poetry;
the shuffle of book-signings is nothing to them.
Let us eat and drink well away from the jostle.

We may be remembered, perhaps by strangers,
but none of us will need to burn our lines.
These days we say what we like, even
in Russia, as if no one is truly listening.
Here in the South, Ireland is eerily booming.

Bells

Big Ben sounds cold tonight.
Each strike an ache of ice.
My neck feels every gong
as a chill. The traffic halts
and the radio news has
a wartime, childhood voice.

Bong. An honourable war,
and simple politics. *Bong.*
We sit in the car and absorb
the rhetoric of peace.
And I remember VE day,
jiving with friendly Yanks,

or sitting in the cinema
applauding Russian tanks.
Bong. Dead bodies fill
our telly screen. Who will
suggest a remedy? For God
was not the Commandmant

who set up Uncle Jo's Gulag
or sent Emma Lazarus' children off
to napalm gooks across Vietnam.
We did it. *Bong.* The human ape,
inheritor of planet earth, and
from our power there's no escape.

Gypsies

'Those black eyed children begging in Bucharest
are all pickpockets,' smiled our exquisite hostess,
who had set a table for us with fresh cucumber,
and sliced tomatoes. 'From the country,' she explained
the delicacy, rare in present-day Rumania.

Crossing the gaunt and treeless plain near Craiova,
We noticed houses painted like caravans,
With curving roofs and colours quaintly Asian.
Our driver said they were owned by rich Gypsies,
'They go to East Germany and steal Mercedes.'

'You know, Gypsies are hated over there,'
I mused to my London newsagent, looking at
a headline about stowaways caught in Dover.
But he, with his sad Pakistani eyes, replied,
'Why are they so hated? They must be bad.'

Revolutions

If you've seen Pontecorvo's *Battle of Algiers*,
you'll remember: the bombs ticking in French cafés
while babies lick ice-cream, the FLN bodies hanging
their heads dunked in urinals, everything
black and white like documentary footage.
The film took the *Lion D'Or* in '66.

All through the fifties, we puzzled at French officers
using torture, wasn't Colonel Mathieu a member
of the old Resistance? Yet they behaved like Nazis.
Our children would be amazed at our innocence,
but they were babies then, or unborn, and nowadays
television has educated everyone in the commonplace

ubiquity of cruelty, the logic of it. It's become
a disgusting part of what we see as human.
So the Algerian Revolution was finally won
but men gave their lives to displace one tyranny
and had it replaced by another. It may be those
most willing to die make their point, but where's the victory?

Gluttony

A ballad after the manner of Bert Brecht

Now people say we ought to curb our appetite –
Unhealthy eating has to be abhorred;
And yet we savour each illicit, risky bite
Of dangerous delights we can't afford.
For only pride dictates we should be thin
Whatever choice we make will be a sin.

Our bodies may be damaged eating too much fat
So, to be safe, what we prefer to choose
Will not occlude this or be furring that.
There's precious little else that we refuse.
Mushrooms and rocket salad, with a tin
Of caviar is quite a modest sin.

To Marks and Spencers' finest new emporium
We travel through the winter's dark to buy
Red salmon eggs, or breast of leanest duck in plum,
Whatever luxuries they can supply.
Addiction to these pleasures is a sin
Less dodgy than a shot of heroin.

At rich relations' tables we sometimes enjoy
Foie gras of goose with port and caramel
Or sushi salmon delicately spiced with soy,
Thick white asparagus that's buttered well.
These are the perks reluctant Duty wins.
Why should we need to speak of them as sins?

We relish halibut in cream and cognac –
Honey glazed sea bass with a crisp white wine.
Although the sweets are more than we can knock back –
Only a sour curmudgeon would decline.
In my politeness, I'm a heroine.
Who can describe such courtesy as sin?

Our glittering consumer world depends on it,
Since where there's profit, nothing is malign;
Moreover, all the food we eat will turn to shit,
A useful link in Nature's Grand Design.
If you pretend that Gluttony's a sin
Forgive me, but I can't repress a grin . . .

Unless there sits outside the supermarket door
Some homeless wreck who shivers in his hunger
I give him my small change, and sometimes more –
My conscience, I suppose, that old scaremonger.
Is he a loser, so the rest can win,
Or is that reassuring thought a sin?

Splitting

To slash, split, open or break.
To sever or smash or crack.
The word for leaving a partner amounts
to violent dismemberment,
yet others perform the act.

So is it courage she lacks?
Is she held by compassion – or fear?
Does she want to believe if
she gambles on going, he'll
wait for her to come back?

Powerbook. Disks. All packed.
His shrink told her years ago:
'He can give you nothing. Try
to detach yourself if you can.' So why
does she go on loving the man?

Poet

The last days of October were dark and wet.
In our London street, a brown rain flooded
the gutters with fallen leaves, and at night
a wind shook the branches of the trees
like a child's rattle. In the countryside,
rivers poured into village houses.

The weather got into our dreams in the figure
of Ted Hughes. One of us, asleep in a chair,
spent the night wandering round his
Devon house, staring through
picture windows in the storm, unable
to find a way outside.

In my mind, he was standing in our old
Cambridge kitchen, his face like mountain stone,
his presence solemn and kind. He bestowed
a gift of abalone shells, without ceremony.
This morning, on the telephone,
his sister called to tell us he had died.

It was almost as if his spirit
in its passing, had casually touched
a synapse. He never needed to stir
to draw attention in a room, the magnet
of his being pulled everyone to him;
now his after-image flashed within us.

We travelled through fields of mud
towards North Tawton Church and funeral,
seeing wet dogs and hovering birds
as he had: all creatures of a brutal
planet, to be observed with love, knowing
their cruelties include the human animal.

Jeopardy

All year I've watched the velvet glow
of your happiness, seen you flow
towards him, while he bathes in your spirit;
a glittering exchange of tongue and wit.
I've known what you wanted most was
the risk of giving without calculation.

Now he consumes your pleasure along
with grapes, tree fungus, red nectar,
and since he is no ordinary sailor,
takes the island for his own, as he
receives your enchanted songs.
Calypso, Calypso,

What he gives in return is splendour:
partly his own, and partly the mirror
in which you perceive your own beauty:
the sum of everything he ever loved.
Relishing the energy of his self-concern,
you have already forgiven his onward journey.

Passion

After Rainer Maria Rilke's 'Abishag'

1

She lay, and let her childish arms be bound
by servants round the dried up body of the king;
her limbs spread on him sweetly all night long.
She found his withered flesh was frightening,

but turned her face into his beard, whenever
a owl hooted, or she heard any other
of the noises that belong to night. Terror
and desire both gathered in her.

The stars throbbed, as if they were fellow victims.
Through the bedchamber a certain smell rose,
and a curtain stirred as if giving a signal.
She tried to understand what it could mean.

She held herself against that dark old man,
with no black moment reached, throughout the night,
a virgin, over failing royal flesh,
still pure, and yet with all her soul alight.

2

All through the empty day the king had been
mulling over what he'd done, and what had
missed out on, petting his dog as he brooded.
Then, in the evening, there was Abishag
arching over him. And suddenly the whole mess
of his past had to be laid aside, so he could sail
that dangerous sea-coast, lying beneath
the twin stars of her silent breasts.

Once an experienced lover of women,
he recognised her unkissed mouth was
unmoved, and that the inner being between
the fork of her flesh felt no desire for him.
He shivered, as he tried to summon up his
last blood, nevertheless, like a dog on a command.

A Former Lover
After Pushkin

Beneath the blue skies of her own country
      she grew sick and withered . . .
Even now, perhaps, somewhere above me
      her young ghost still hovers,
while I am numb, and this final separation
      rouses no more pain in me
than in the lips that, just now, calmly
      gave the news of her death.

Yet she was someone I once loved with passion,
      and all the usual anxieties:
tension, tenderness, unhappiness
      reaching almost to madness;
where has all that torment disappeared? Sadly,
      for her too trusting spirit, see,
all the sweet memory of days gone by stirs
      neither a tear nor reproach in me.